LIBRARY
Davies Career & Technical H.S.
Lincoln, R.I. 02865

D1776187

Lessons from the SAMURAI

Ancient Self-Defense Strategies and Techniques

Lessons from the SAMURAI
Ancient Self-Defense Strategies and Techniques

Fred Neff
Photographs by Bob Wolfe

Lerner Publications Company • Minneapolis

The models photographed in this book are Richard DeValerio, John H. Wong, Michelle Wong, Michael C. Wong, Andre Richardson, Jim Reid, and Douglas Shrewsbury.

LIBRARY OF CONGRESS CATALOGING-IN-PUBLICATION DATA

Neff, Fred.
  Lessons from the samurai.

  Includes index.
  Summary: Explains the history and philosophy of Japan's samurai warriors and describes basic samurai self-defense techniques, which include jujitsu, judo, and kendo.
  1. Martial arts—Japan—Juvenile literature. 2. Self-defense—Japan—Juvenile literature. 3. Samurai—Juvenile literature. [1. Martial arts. 2. Self-defense. 3. Samurai] I. Wolfe, Robert L., ill. II. Title. III. Series.
  GV1100.77.A2N44   1986   796.8′1′0952   86-21118
  ISBN 0-8225-1161-4 (lib. bdg.)

Copyright © 1987 by Lerner Publications Company

All rights reserved. International copyright secured. No part of this book may be reproduced in any form whatsoever without permission in writing from the publisher except for the inclusion of brief quotations in an acknowledged review.

Manufactured in the United States of America

International Standard Book Number: 0-8225-1161-4
Library of Congress Catalog Card Number: 86-21118

To my special friend, Christa Ruth Powell, who has stood by me through adversity and hardship with unwavering optimism and loyalty.

CONTENTS

	Preface	9
1	History	11
2	Philosophy	17
3	Common Questions	23
4	Conditioning the Body for Battle	27
5	Meditation	39
6	Foundation for Defense: Stances	41
7	Movement and Dodging	45
8	The Art of Atemi	51
9	Punches and Strikes	53
10	Foot Techniques	61
11	Blocks	65
12	Combinations	69
13	The Art of Throwing	75
14	Escapes and Counters	89
15	Containment Strategy	101
16	Safety Considerations	109
	Index	111

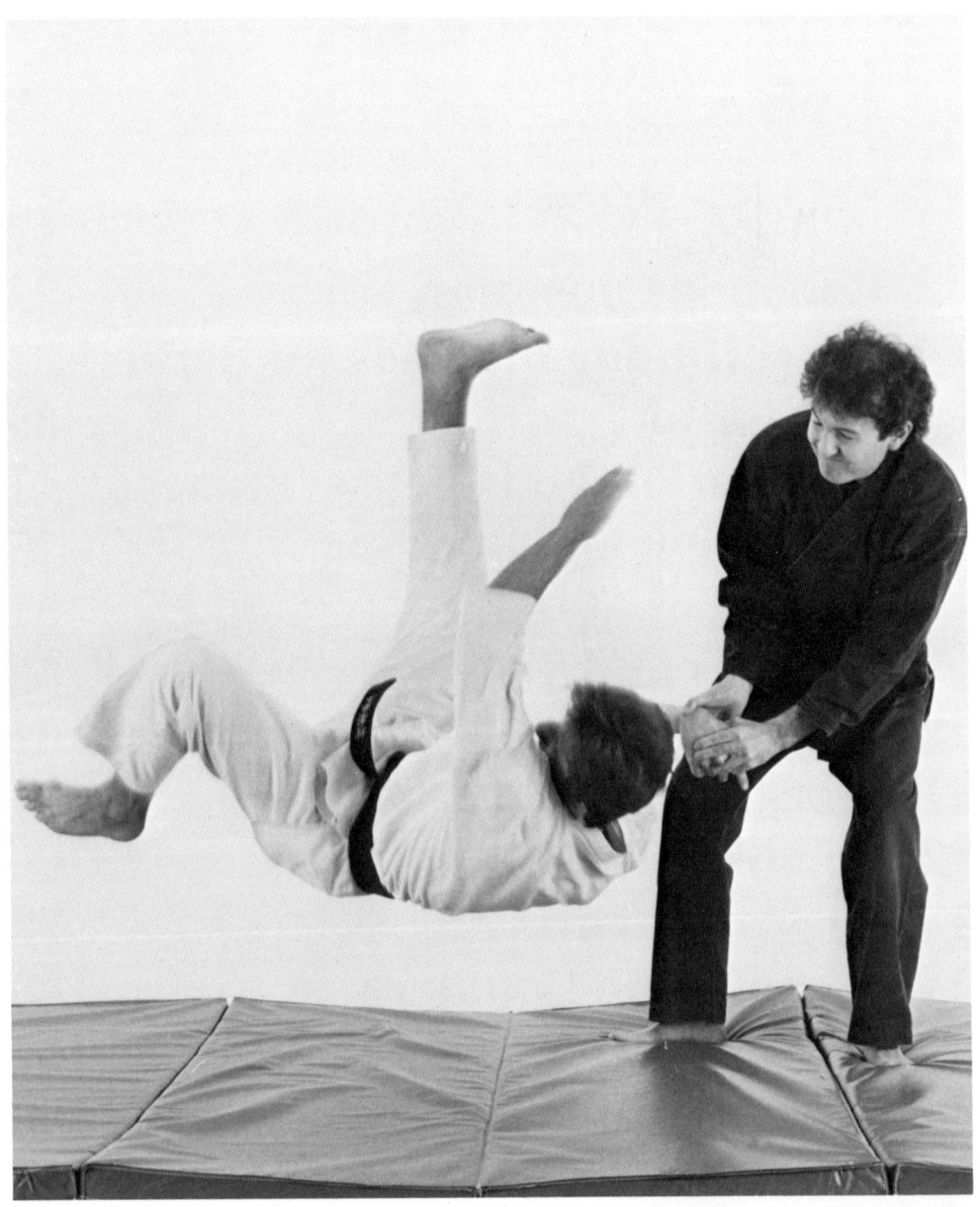

PREFACE

Two armor-clad warriors face one another with an almost empty stare. They stand with swords raised over their heads, ready to strike in an instant. Suddenly, one swings his sword—and is caught by surprise when the adversary's sword strikes first.

Similar scenes appear often on television or in the movies. But even without this media exposure, it is not surprising that the general public has many questions about these warriors— the samurai.

I was first introduced to samurai fighting methods while studying combat jujitsu. Jujitsu is a form of self-defense designed to be used in real-life fighting situations. Jujitsu techniques rely on knowledge of the way the human body works and the use of an opponent's own momentum and force against him. As I learned the art, I wondered how this form of fighting had developed. However, the intense training sessions I attended taught only the techniques, and none of the art's history.

In 1963, a local YMCA offered a course in judo. I signed up for it in order to learn more about judo and its relationship to jujitsu. The major emphasis of the class was on physical fitness and learning how to fall. Our only lesson on history was a short session explaining how the samurai warriors' art of jujitsu had led to judo. This whetted my appetite to learn more about the samurai and their forms of fighting. I asked questions whenever possible. I studied whatever was available on the subject. Over time I realized that one could study the samurai and their methods of fighting for a lifetime without learning more than a fraction of their ways.

Samurai philosophy and methods have had a great impact on both the Eastern and Western worlds in the twentieth century. From samurai fighting methods and related ways of thought have come the popular modern arts of kendo (sword fighting), judo, and jujitsu.

The samurai philosophy has possibly an even greater effect on society today than in ancient times because its followers have spread from Japan throughout the world. The samurai taught methods of planning, an understanding of the universe, how to handle critical moments of stress, and human relations.

The values and beliefs of the samurai warriors set the pace for modern Japan's industrial might. The warriors' philosophy of dedication, motivation and action are part of the work ethic of Japan. Scratch the surface of large firms in Japan and you will find something of the samurai way of thought. The *Bushido* code is still active in revised form as an underlying thinking pattern for thousands of successful individuals.

This book will introduce you to the samurai and provide basic lessons from their philosophy and methods.

This book covers unarmed methods to contain and control an attacker's force. Unarmed methods are more useful than swordplay for modern self-defense. Readers who want to continue studying may learn many more of the samurai's jujitsu techniques by studying with a qualified instructor. No matter how much or how little you study the samurai, I am sure you will find them fascinating. The samurai stand for a level of human achievement that we could all aspire to. Some of the principles they lived by are still useful and valid today.

It is suggested that you slowly and carefully read each chapter. Try to think not only about the physical techniques, but also about the philosophy behind them. Do not rush your study, but concentrate on improving. Try not to move to the next technique until you can do the current one smoothly and with proper form. It is better to know a few techniques and understand them than to have a loose idea of many methods. You can depend on a fighting technique only if you can do it instantaneously, and the ability to react instantly comes from a great deal of practice. Lessons of the samurai are valid today and can be very rewarding if you practice regularly and with strict attention to detail. I hope you enjoy the lessons from the samurai as much as I have.

1
HISTORY

The samurai art of unarmed combat predates the samurai class itself. The ancient Japanese practiced a form of wrestling which later developed into *sumai,* or "struggle." Sumai contributed techniques to sumo wrestling, jujitsu, and judo. In ancient days it was a tough form of combat. In a sumai battle, the goal was to make the opponent surrender unconditionally. Fighting was at close range, with grappling, striking, kicking and butting all allowed.

The evolving Japanese warrior class, the *bushi,* took fighting techniques from sumai to supplement their weapons, and then added other fighting methods. Each large group of bushi developed its own distinct fighting strategy. By the sixteenth century, there were many blends of unarmed combat in Japan.

Over time, the bushi developed into warriors, administrators, and philosophers. Before the ninth century, Japanese culture centered around an emperor, who was believed by many to be the descendent of a Japanese god. The emperor's loyal bushi helped him run the government and military forces. Gradually, between the ninth and eleventh centuries, the word samurai came to be applied to the class of people who served nobility or powerful political chieftains. To this day, some translate the Japanese word samurai to mean "those who serve."

After a time, the imperial family became less important, while those who served them increased in power. For almost three centuries, samurai groups or clans fought for power, causing almost constant civil war. One group would gain control of the country, then its decline would begin and new warfare would break out. Whenever a particular group took power, their leader was called *shogun.* In theory, the shogun reported to the emperor, but in reality he was the military head of government and had very broad power. Government districts were ruled by local leaders called *daimyo,* who reported to the shogun. Each daimyo kept trained samurai warriors that owed allegiance to him and fought for him.

The constant warfare led to even greater emphasis on fighting methods. The samurai were usually expected to be effective fighters in at least a couple of types of defense, such as the bow, the spear, the sword, or hand-to-hand combat. Later, firearms were added to the list of weapons. Most important was the sword, which became a symbol of the samurai class.

Many years of hard training and suffering were needed to develop the balance, timing, and self-control required to use the sword properly. Mental preparation was also a major ingredient of the training. A battle involved not only physical skills, but the ability to control emotions. For example, samurai swordsmen would stand facing one another within striking distance and wait for the other person to make the first move. Sometimes it was quite a while before either man acted. The better person would be the one who could strike the other person's body so as to disable him. The key was to be loose, yet not so relaxed that concentration was eased for even a brief moment.

The emphasis on swordplay had a great effect on many other facets of samurai existence. In the early years of the bushi, Japanese warriors had emphasized the bow and arrow. This caused the gradual development of protective armor. Archers often fought on horseback. Their armor consisted of small plates of metal that were overlapped and tied together with colored straps. As time went by, the samurai often had to fight on rough, wooded, and mountainous terrain, where it was difficult to remain on horseback. The bow and arrow was slowly abandoned, along with heavy armor. Light, flexible armor that gave more freedom of movement when fighting with swords was developed. Later, in peaceful times, armor further evolved into very ornate dress uniforms, now recognized as works of art.

At the same time as the samurai became a power in Japan, another fighting class arose: the warrior monks. Many of the Japanese temples, facing the growing power of samurai clans, encouraged their members to train in martial arts. They also recruited samurai to become monks. During the eleventh and twelfth centuries, warrior monks were an especially formidable force.

Fighting techniques were often exchanged between samurai and monk. The monks taught their warriors to have no fear of war and this greatly affected the samurai philosophy. Many samurai sought to emulate the monks' confidence and, therefore, to be admirable in thought and action.

In the thirteenth century, the samurai class experienced a new, heightened interest in religion. Many samurai began to accept Zen Buddhism. This type of Buddhism encouraged individual study and growth. People who embraced a Zen way of life were expected to undergo very tough physical, mental, emotional, and spiritual training. Zen played a large part in developing the samurai's ability to undergo extremes of hardship and pain without complaint. A samurai philosophy developed, based in part on Zen. It taught warriors to be willing to accept death and to have

almost no fear of fighting. The samurai ideals eventually permeated Japanese art and culture as well. The customs, art and philosophy of this period are part of the foundations of modern Japan.

By the early fifteenth century, the Japanese had achieved extraordinary quality in weapons and armor. Japanese swords became a symbolic weapon, representing the soul of the samurai. A long ritual was developed to ensure the quality of swords. As civil war grew more intense, so did the importance of the sword.

At the same time, weaponless fighting skills were also advancing. By the middle of the 1500s, a positive turning point was reached when Takenouchi Hisamori developed the foundation for modern jujitsu. Other fighting methods were organized and named until eventually there were over 700 jujitsu systems. Chinese *kempo* ("fist way"), brought to Japan by Chinese visitors, may have contributed to Japanese hand-to-hand combat. Some warriors included kempo tactics in their jujitsu practice. These tactics probably affected jujitsu striking and kicking methods more than grappling. Many methods of jujitsu appear to be the exclusive creation of the ancient Japanese.

By the late 1500s, the samurai were so powerful as a class that they were able to remove the right to possess weapons from all the other classes.

A samurai general's armor, made in the early 1800s.

The samurai used as their reason the idea that possession of weapons would lead to unrest and interrupt farming. The real reason was that this put the samurai clearly above everyone else in power and status. The fact that only samurai could wear two swords gave them an exclusive badge of recognition.

In 1603, the Tokugawa era began with the rise of a new shogun to power. From 1603 to 1868, there was general peace in Japan. The tradition of great respect for the samurai and their ways did not end, however. People took pride in bushi ideals and fighting forms. Even though fighting was not needed as before, study of martial arts continued. This was a great age for the development and growth of the use of weapons and hand-to-hand combat. The goverment itself fostered the samurai tradition because it was led by that class.

The fighting techniques were tough combat forms. The term *jujitsu,* or "gentle art," refers to the flexibility of responses and not to the effect of the techniques on an aggressor. Jujitsu was based on the soft or gentle yield. This meant giving way to force, to redirect energy and defeat an attacker. For example, yielding to a strong forward push would cause the attacker's own momentum to throw him off balance. Jujitsu techniques used by the samurai included kicking, punching, butting, throwing, holding locks, grappling techniques and close weaponry.

Later, a second form of jujitsu developed, more oriented toward throws, holds, and general grappling. This form was practiced for physical fitness and ordinary self-defense, not life-or-death struggles. It is referred to as civilian jujitsu, and the early type with life-endangering aspects is called combat jujitsu.

During this peaceful period, some samurai were without work or were not paid by their daimyos. Some made a living by teaching martial arts to others. This passed the skills of the samurai to a larger group of people. However, the large number of samurai who were trained for warfare and without work created a problem which grew increasingly serious. To help keep the ideals of the samurai in their minds and to teach these ideals to others, a written code came into being. It later was called the *Bushido* or "way of the warrior." The samurai role in life and in society was emphasized. The code covered the importance of loyalty, benevolence, politeness, and other social responsibilities. However, even samurai who fully accepted the code were troubled by the awkward position of having the training and attitude of warriors in a country of peace.

During the nineteenth century, certain European influences were allowed into the country. The bushi grew increasingly dissatisfied that their sacred land was being spoiled by people they believed to be barbarians. War broke out in the 1860s. Those who wanted to keep their homeland pure fought against the supporters of the shogun who had allowed in the

Western influence. The shogun's followers were defeated and this ended the Tokugawa era. All the shogun's powers were transferred back to the emperor, the original source. A new era began, called the Meiji restoration after the current emperor. Sweeping changes took place. There was a simplification of the class system, more freedom of occupation, and agricultural reform.

Most significant to the samurai was the fact that common people could be drafted for the army. This ended the samurai's exclusive right to wage war. In the 1870s, a law was passed banning the wearing of swords unless a person was in the military. The samurai's power was gone. Their status was reduced and they had to find other means to earn a living.

The Japanese army became interested in Western military methods and let the samurai fighting arts fade. In an effort to keep the fighting arts alive, the great man Jigoro Kano took those techniques of jujitsu that could be safely used and created the sport of judo. He hoped to not only keep fighting methods alive, but to build people's health and develop their spirits.

Since then, judo has been chosen as a recreation by many people who are interested primarily in sport. Jujitsu was for the most part kept alive by those who wanted effective self-defense methods that had stood the test of time. Although the two arts have a common ancestry, they have distinct objectives.

This book offers lessons in jujitsu similar to those practiced by the samurai. It emphasizes containment techniques, which stop an opponent from aggression without seriously injuring him. Just as the samurai did, the student should temper the fighting techniques with a proper attitude. You can learn many valuable lessons from the samurai if you open your mind and develop your skill in thinking. Possibly even more important than the techniques are the positive ideals and the confidence these ideals give a student. Those who study samurai methods and thoughts will be intrigued by their history, and will become more effective in self-defense, as they can gain insight into themselves and experience personal growth.

2 PHILOSOPHY

The samurai code of ethics has often been called *Bushido*. This has been translated into English as "military man way," or, more commonly, "way of the warrior." This code evolved out of the need to prepare a samurai mentally and emotionally for the rigors of life-or-death struggles. It emphasized constant physical training to develop the fighting techniques and the discipline of character needed to face an attacker without fear or hesitation. Bushido included seven virtues, which can be described as follows:

1. Loyalty

One must have loyalty to one's superiors. This was a foundation of bushi social thinking. Samurai must be willing to follow their leader's cause, even if it put them in an extremely difficult position.

2. Justice

Justice was an important part of the samurai way of life. Samurai were not to act dishonestly or in a manner below their station. Ideas and fighting methods were judged by whether they were just.

3. Courage

To be a samurai, one had to have the courage to act even in the face of almost impossible odds. Experience and training developed the instant reactions that meant courage to face death. A true samurai warrior always moved forward without thought of retreat.

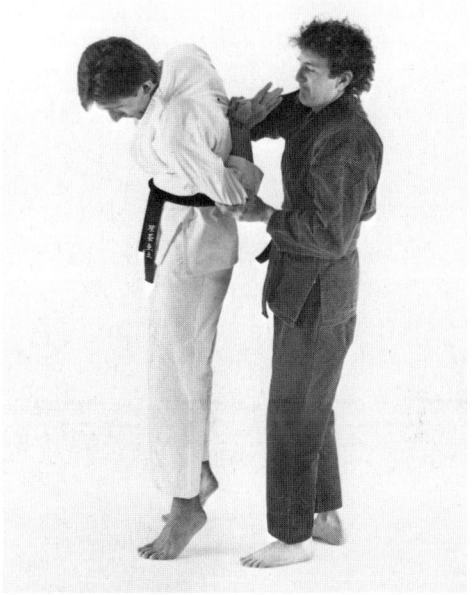

4. Benevolence

This concept included the ability to show love, affection, and sympathy to other people. It is not to be confused with weakness. Benevolence is the proper application of Bushido techniques. Taking wrongful advantage of an opponent would be disgraceful and a violation of the concept of benevolence.

5. Politeness

Proper manner and general politeness were highly valued by the samurai. The polite warrior was thought to exhibit courage, because he showed no fear of other people. The discipline of politeness was believed to build the individual's character while promoting general harmony.

6. Truthfulness

To many samurai, lying was dishonorable. The word of a warrior should be sufficient in any dealings. A true samurai who followed the Bushido code would prize honesty and his word could always be depended upon.

7. Honor

Each samurai's honor and reputation was not important only to him. An assault on a samurai's honor was often considered to be a direct attack on his family and ancestors as well. An attack on one's honor often brought on a duel between the insulted samurai and the offender.

Many of these virtues are still valued and can be extremely useful in developing character. However, keep in mind that each of the seven virtues must be balanced with the others. Too much attention to any one virtue would lead to an unbalanced approach to life.

The seven virtues were often taught to the samurai from birth, along with the way of Zen. The Zen philosophy helped put the virtues in perspective, and gave the samurai confidence for fighting. Zen is a method for approaching life. It stresses the importance of depending on one's self. The Zen philosophy helped the samurai to effectively use new knowledge because it encouraged them to act without reservation and with total commitment.

The samurai believed that if they practiced correctly, they would learn a subconscious pattern that allowed them to perform the correct action almost spontaneously when needed. A warrior who trained hard did not have to think what to do. He could automatically adapt his response to the situation. It is only when a person does not have to think about an activity and remember its steps that one can do it well. This flexibility of action and instant response was prized.

The samurai learned in two types of practice, the passive way of contemplation during relaxation, and the active way of physical exercise. Training that did not include both of these was considered by the samurai to be incomplete. To the samurai, fighting was a part of life. Therefore, their training simply prepared them to live harmoniously within nature's rules. One needed a relaxed period to prepare for the great amount of energy needed in the physical activity of training or combat.

The samurai believed the best way to learn was with a clear mind, with no preconceived ideas. This meant that the warrior should not question a new technique until he had practiced it enough to know whether it was effective for him.

The samurai believed that no matter what the challenge, there was nothing that could not be overcome. To win, one must focus on the purpose and move ahead without hesitation.

They were always open to improving their knowledge of weaponry, fighting techniques, or philosophy. If they discovered a useful insight in Chinese, Indian, or Buddhist thought, they incorporated it into their lives. This admirable trait of openness helped build Japan into a world leader in the twentieth century.

Samurai training attempted to develop the whole person. It was recognized that a samurai with the best of weapons would perform poorly if he felt fear, or had worries or self-doubts. Therefore, conditioning was mental, physical, and spiritual.

Special training from an early age developed spirit, the fire inside a person. The samurai realized that what was important was not the technique or the weapon, but the person. Elements of spirit such as willpower, self-control, courage, commitment, and ability to withstand pressure were developed.

The samurai taught that complete unity of the mind, body, and spirit will make a person unbeatable. There is a samurai saying that the greatest warrior is the one who conquers himself. Although samurai training was varied and sophisticated, there were certain key principles that can be learned and applied today. These principles are:

1. Remain calm.

Prepare yourself for the task at hand by remaining calm and focusing on what is happening in front of you. Do not pay attention to any illusion the opponent is trying to create, but instead watch for his or her real strengths and weaknesses. The samurai believed that everyone looks, but the successful fighter sees what is happening, even if it is something he or she does not want to see. Often people ignore a situation because they do not want to face it. The illusion they create in their minds causes even bigger problems later. In a practical sense, many times a person does not spot aggression until he or she is harmed. The samurai insight into what is happening is a key to success. Once you conquer fear, worry, and illusions, you will have a great part of the battle won.

2. Clear the mind of self-doubt.

The samurai realized a person's self-concept is a key to his or her success. *Mushin* is a word used by the Japanese which has been translated as "no-mindedness," or "without thinking." What it really refers to is the ability to avoid a negative self-concept. By clearing the mind and letting no self-doubt creep in, the samurai or

student can execute techniques gracefully, quickly, and efficiently. The ultimate aim in training is to learn not to put any emotional barriers in your way. Self-consciousness and self-doubt are the enemies of effectiveness. The first step in developing mushin is to relax and clear your mind for action. Realize you can do something, and thereafter do not concentrate on yourself at all. You will find that without self-doubt, your actions will be extremely effective.

3. Be positive.

Assume a positive mental position and do not think defeat. Take a strong body position, looking forward with the confidence that expresses success. This physical and mental state will be seen by your opponent as a sign of danger. If you think you are good and act that way, you will succeed. Once a fight begins, spot your opening quickly, close in, and strike. Do not hesitate or allow your opponent time to regroup. The samurai believed hesitation often leads to defeat.

4. Hold back nothing.

Makoto is a samurai concept of action. It is often translated as "sincerity," but in a sense this does not give full justice to the concept. To the samurai it meant that one must put everything into any act. All of your heart, spirit, mind and physical strength should be put in, and nothing held back. Also, it meant there should be no hesitation in the act. When you obey this concept, your power is tremendous.

5. Center on a single purpose.

The samurai were conditioned to strike with *isshin,* or one mind. This meant tackling any situation, task, or even battle with focused concentration. When you do this, all of your power, strength and ability can be translated into the task. Most individuals only use a small part of their ability on any task because they are distracted by outside factors. One of the best lessons the martial arts can teach is focusing the mind onto a single purpose. Learn to become a totally committed person. If you put all your energy behind something, success is assured.

6. Use an attacker's own energy to defeat him or her.

The samurai believed that sometimes one could win by rolling with a person's attack, blending your opponent's attack into your counterattack. Instead of blocking an attack, one directed it further in the direction it was going. Once the opponent is overextended, he defeats himself. This allows you to take advantage of your opponent's power. The more aggressively your opponent pushes, the easier it is for you to pull him or her off balance. The key, then, is not who is more powerful, but who is more capable of directing the other's energy to control the situation. This rule of strategy can be applied, not only in fighting, but in a variety of other situations.

7. Take advantage of opportunity.

Suki has been translated as "a space between two objects where something else can enter," or "a gap in the fighter's attention." Suki is an unguarded moment. Find your own weaknesses and practice defenses to cover them. Everyone has gaps in their defenses, and the better you are at finding your own in training, the less likely an opponent can take advantage of them to harm you. Likewise, look for a gap in your opponent's defense. Once you have spotted it, quickly take advantage of the unguarded spot.

8. Be persistent and anything can be conquered.

There is a concept, called *kufu*, which applies equally to small, everyday tasks and to large problems in life. It means giving yourself completely to finding a solution. It literally means to struggle or wrestle until you can conquer a problem. One must learn to kufu with a problem, to stay with it and try again and again to overcome it.

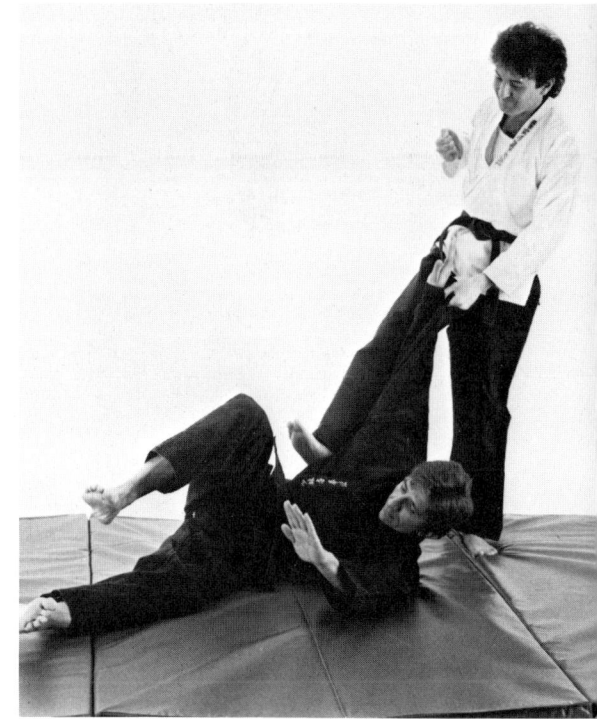

3 COMMON QUESTIONS

1. How can samurai training teach me how to fight without also brutalizing my attitude toward others?

The samurai philosophy strongly emphasises discipline and persistence in training. Only strong discipline and persistent training can give a warrior the spontaneous skills needed to be an effective fighter. Out of this vigorous training comes the ability to meet aggression instantly. The response is automatic, without anger or intent to harm. Fighting techniques are used only when attacked. You act not to harm the adversary but merely to contain the aggression. Once the attacker's force is controlled, all action stops.

When you are confident that you can stop any attack almost automatically, you do not have to brag or bully. Instead, you can enjoy life without having to prove yourself to others. This is the the goal of this book: to bring out self-confidence without aggressiveness.

2. What types of physical conditioning are needed for jujitsu?

Your exercise program should include general flexibility training, strength building and activities to build the cardiovascular system for endurance. Start with slow stretches to make the body more pliable for training. Exercises for strength, such as push-ups and pull-ups, may be performed next. Then move into the practice of jujitsu techniques. Aerobic exercises to build wind make a useful follow-up to the main training program. Activities such as swimming, running, cycling, and walking are useful. At the end of each exercise session, there should be a regular cooling-down period of stretches.

3. I have always been plagued by worry. Did the samurai have any techniques to help me conquer this problem?

The first step in conquering worry is to realize that it is only fear about something that might happen in the future. Many times you worry for nothing, since the event you fear never happens. When you concentrate on worry, it hurts you inside while predisposing you to accept the feared event. When your energy is directed more toward action and less toward worry, the fear soon disappears. In addition to acting to solve specific problems, a pattern of calisthenics, seated meditation, and self-defense training also helps cut down on worry.

4. Where did the samurai get their philosophy?

The samurai philosophy was a combination of the teachings of Confucius, the Shinto religion, and Zen Buddhism. Confucius taught certain ethics in dealing with people and institutions. Shintoism continued the tradition of respect and reverence for nature and its ways. Zen taught principles of mental discipline and spiritual and physical development.

5. I have always been afraid to assert myself because it might lead to a fight. Is there any way I can lose my fear?

Fear is concentration on all of the negative things that can happen. When you start to believe that you can do something well, you will not fear a bad outcome. The first step in doing away with fear is acceptance of the idea that the samurai techniques will work for you. This means you have no need to fear. It is important to concentrate on an aggressor's weaknesses and your general fighting strategy, rather than on the possibility of injury. Often the aggressor has just as much fear of harm, if not more, than you. If you remain calm and concentrate on what you are doing, your attitude will impress the aggressor and make him or her feel that you have the strength and power to win. The aggressor's response may be to give up.

To condition yourself so that fear is not a factor in determining whether you fight, do the following:

Make up your mind that you are a strong fighter. If needed, repeat this over and over to yourself until you accept it.

Practice the techniques continually until they have become second nature. If you can respond automatically in any situation, you will defend yourself without having time to doubt. A by-product of this is that you will have great confidence, knowing that you can automatically move into action if necessary.

Practice the techniques with a partner to simulate a real fight, so that you feel confident when facing another person.

Keep in mind that bullies are people who have a tremendous amount of fear and self-doubt, so they have to prove themselves by picking on someone they think they can defeat.

Remember that a little fear is not always a bad thing. It may give you the energy to launch an attack and keep you from becoming so relaxed that you are caught off guard.

6. In what ways are the samurai fighting arts different from karate?

Samurai unarmed fighting arts derive from a combination of the ancient Japanese grappling techniques such as sumai and the Chinese influence of kempo. Many schools of practical self-defense came out of these sources. The various systems put emphasis on different techniques. In general, however, they shared a common goal, which was to use hand-to-hand fighting techniques to supplement weapons when fighters were close and could not use sword, bow, spear, or other weapon. These were the fighting arts of nobility and were primarily used by them. They were extremely effective combat techniques that were not for sport or artistic demonstrations.

Karate came from the island of Okinawa where the people developed it to defend against the raids of pirates and the attempted conquest by samurai warriors. Because the Okinawans were not allowed to use weapons, they developed an art that would allow them to fight either empty-handed or with ordinary tools. Over time, various families of empty-hand techniques developed. Each of these schools was extremely effective and put a heavy emphasis on punching and kicking techniques. The Japanese brought the art to Japan around the turn of the century. Over time, it came to be called *karate,* meaning "empty-hand way."

Both the samurais' jujitsu and the Okinawans' karate have effective techniques for self-defense. They differ, however, in their emphasis. Jujitsu relies more on close fighting and grappling, whereas karate emphasises powerful hand and foot techniques thrown from a long range. However, each art has certain techniques similar to the other.

7. Is there any secret to the dynamic throws of the samurai?

There is no secret, just practice of proper technique. The key is to perform the throwing movement on

an opponent who is off-balance. An aggressive bully often breaks his or her own balance simply by making the first move. For example, an opponent who tries to push you backward will usually put his or her weight on the balls of the feet. The opponent could then be easily thrown forward because the person's balance is broken in that direction. You can prepare for a throw by learning to push or pull when your opponent makes a movement that puts him or her off balance. In the later chapters, where throws are taught, directing the opponent off balance is usually done in the first two or three movements of the technique.

25

8. Did the samurai have any moves that I can easily learn to destroy an opponent?

Deadly moves are not taught in this book because they are not necessary or consistent with the basic philosophy of jujitsu. Brutality was never condoned by the samurai. Instead, self-defense was applied only where justice and honor demanded it. To provoke a fight or to do unnecessary damage to an opponent was not respected. A person should not intend to do great harm, but should act in response to another's aggression. However, sometimes it may be necessary to attack. If faced off against someone who is clearly dangerous, you may have to move forward and attack to beat the opponent to the punch. But you should never purposely start a confrontation or do unnecessary harm.

9. I have tried martial arts training before, but could not stick with it because it seemed too hard to learn. Do you have suggestions on how I can stay with my training?

Tackle training, or, for that matter, any major task, as a challenge. Set periodic goals in training to keep yourself interested. Try to relax each day by meditating. Keep in mind when you get discouraged that people have limitless capacities to learn and to do just about anything, if they are willing to put out the effort. You may not start out as the most coordinated or even the fastest learner, but if you are persistent, you will become skillful. Sometimes you perceive a difficulty that is not really there. Once you get started you may realize the task is enjoyable and you can succeed. Focus on your purpose, put all your power of concentration behind it, and be willing to struggle with the problem through good and bad times, and you will accomplish more than you think you can.

10. What is the secret of the samurai's amazing power called *"ki"*?

The samurai believed that in order to gain proper strength and power, one must focus on the development of *ki*. Its equivalent in Chinese martial arts is *chi*. There is no word in the English language to convey the full meaning of ki. It is a special kind of energy, vitality, breath, and life force that can be harnessed to make life more meaningful and the individual more effective. Ki is developed by proper training in how the body works and in breathing methods. People who have learned how to breathe properly and use their own bodies correctly increase their energy. As a result they feel better and more relaxed and are more effective in their techniques. It takes a great deal of time, patience, practice, and dedication to develop ki. Those who seriously desire ki should seek instruction from a qualified martial arts instructor.

4
CONDITIONING THE BODY FOR BATTLE

The samurai had a saying: "What we do in today's practice prepares for tomorrow's battles." The samurai believed in conditioning the mind, body, and spirit. Practice was constant and hard. However, today people live sedentary lives. You must therefore be very careful to be in proper physical condition before attempting to practice any self-defense moves. If you are not in proper shape, you could easily injure yourself. No matter how good you are at a technique, if you do not have proper conditioning, flexibility, or endurance, you may be missing a key ingredient to surviving a confrontation. As you become more physically fit, your mind will respond more quickly and more effectively, and your outlook will be more positive.

In order to prepare you for battle and to generally make you more fit, a variety of exercises is covered in this chapter. Included are exercises to teach you how to fall, so you can prepare for the practice of throwing techniques. The exercises in this chapter are not the only useful ones for conditioning, but form a basic core you can add to later.

You should always stretch for at least twenty minutes before practicing. Your body needs to warm up and limber up before going through strenuous training. It is suggested that you perform the exercises in the order given below to get maximum conditioning with a minimum of injury.

Neck Conditioner

Stand erect with your feet slightly apart and your arms hanging loosely at your sides. Drop your chin toward your chest, and slowly roll your head in a circle in one direction. After completing a circle in one direction, roll the other way. Do at least four circles in each direction.

Toe Touches

Stand erect with your feet together and your arms hanging loosely at your sides. Reach both arms above your head, then reach down and try to touch the ground. Keep your legs nearly straight, but reach down only until your muscles resist. Don't force it. Repeat the exercise at least ten times.

Basic Side Stretch

Stand erect with your feet apart. Place your left hand on your hip and reach and stretch with your right hand as far to your left as you can. Straighten up, then stretch to the right. Stretch to each side three times.

Body-Twisting Exercise

Stand with your feet apart and your knees slightly bent. Hold your arm bent at the elbow at chest level. Twist at the waist as far as you can comfortably go to the left, then to the right. Repeat in each direction at least four times.

Basic Two-Leg Stretch

Stand erect with your feet spread slightly apart. Slowly spread your legs as far apart as possible without straining the muscles. The basic two-leg stretch should be learned gradually so that the leg muscles are not damaged. Do it only once during each exercise session.

Basic Wall Push-Up

Place the palms of your hands against a solid object and move your feet at least three feet away from it. Bend your elbows, bringing your chest close to the object. Hold that position for at least a count of twenty-five.

Basic Back-Stretching Exercise

Lie on your back with your knees bent and your feet flat on the ground. Put your hand behind your left knee and bring your leg as close to your chest as possible. Do not pull hard; do it slowly and gradually. Return to your original position and repeat the procedure with your other leg. Do the exercise ten times with each leg.

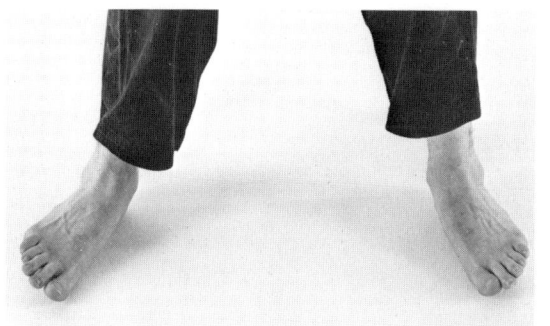

Ankle Conditioners

NOTE: Consult with a doctor before attempting any ankle-stretching exercise if you have stiff ankles or a history of ankle injury.

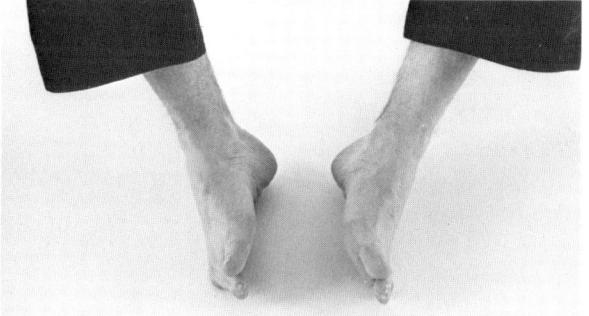

Sit with your weight supported so your feet just touch the ground. Turn your ankles gently outward and hold for a count of ten. Relax. Slowly and gradually turn your ankles inward and hold for a count of ten. Do not force any motion, but allow your ankles to move gently as far as they can. Relax. Turn your toes downward and hold for a count of ten, then relax. Turn your toes upward as far as they can go without forcing it. Hold for a count of ten, then relax. Repeat each action at least twice with each foot.

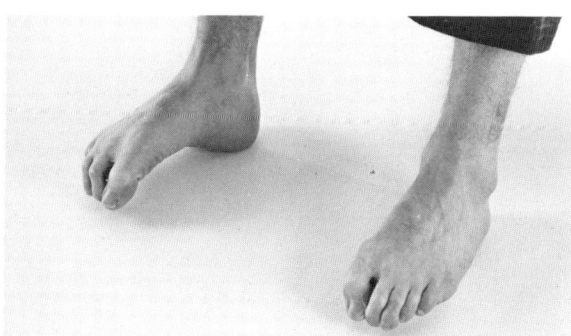

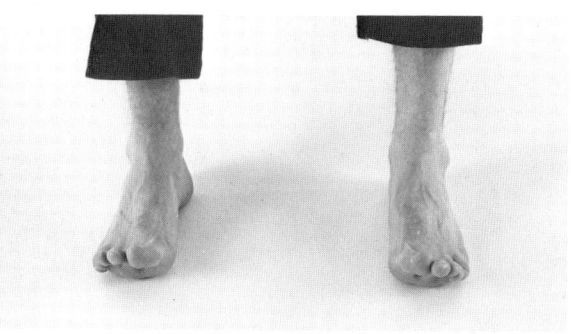

Wrist Circle

NOTE: If you have arthritis or any other condition that weakens or stiffens joints, do not practice joint locks. The wrist is sensitive and easily injured. It is suggested that any wrist joint exercises be practiced at first under the supervision of a qualified instructor.

Roll your wrist in a circle, bending your hand back as far as you can without pain or discomfort. Rotate each wrist first in one direction and then in the other. It is important for the joint to become loose and pliable so that you are not easily injured in practice. Never force any wrist action.

Basic Wrist Stretch

Do this exercise only after your body is warmed up. It should be done as a follow-up to the wrist circle exercise, not a replacement. This is an optional exercise, for use by those who are practicing wrist locks.

Very gently bend your wrist backward as far as you can without any pain. Hold the position for a count of two and release. Bend your hand forward as far as you can without discomfort and hold for a count of two, then release. Be extremely careful not to force the action.

Basic Wrist, Hand, and Forearm Conditioner

Hold a small, rubber ball in the palm of your hand. Squeeze the ball as hard as you can and hold for a count of two, then release. Start by performing this exercise five times with each hand. Gradually build up until you can squeeze the ball and hold it for a count of five for at least twenty-five repetitions.

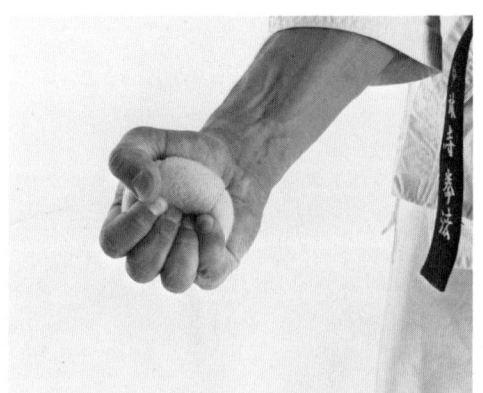

FALLING EXERCISES

The samurai were very careful to safeguard against injury in close combat. They developed certain falling techniques that protected them from harm. Correct falling techniques have saved many a warrior from being injured in combat. If you know how to fall correctly, you will be less vulnerable to injury when you are thrown or tripped by an attacker. You will also gain confidence because you will not fear being thrown. Learning how to fall properly is an essential part of training. The following are beginning falling techniques that students can practice under supervision until they become second nature. As students advance in studies under a qualified instructor, they will be introduced to additional techniques such as landing on the feet.

When practicing falling, obey the following safety rules:
1. Always practice on a large, thick mat in order to protect yourself from injury. NEVER practice on a hard surface.
2. Always do stretching exercises for at least twenty minutes before beginning practice, so your body is loose and flexible.
3. Do each falling technique slowly at first. This will give you a chance to develop proper form. Never speed up the movement until you have mastered the proper form.
4. At first, perform falling exercises under the supervision of a qualified instructor. DO NOT allow anyone to throw you until your falling skills are excellent.

Rear Fall

This fall is used when you are thrown or knocked off balance so that you fall directly backward. Begin in a squatting stance with your knees slightly bent. Extend your arms directly in front of you and tuck in your chin. Spring up from your knees and allow your body to fall backward. As you fall, extend your arms out to either side of your body. Just before your back hits the mat, break your fall by slapping your forearms against the mat about six inches (15 centimeters) from either side of your body. Your head should not touch the mat at any point during the fall.

Side Fall

This is one of the more common falling techniques. It is an effective way to avoid injury when you are thrown over an opponent's hip, shoulder, or leg. Start in a squatting position with one leg crossed in front of the other. Gradually slide your front leg forward. This should cause you to lose your balance and fall on your side. As you fall, bring your arm up in the air. Just before you hit the mat, beat the palm of your raised hand against the mat to break your fall. It is important that your body lands properly, so the knees, ankles and other sensitive spots are not injured. Make sure that after you land, your body is in the position illustrated.

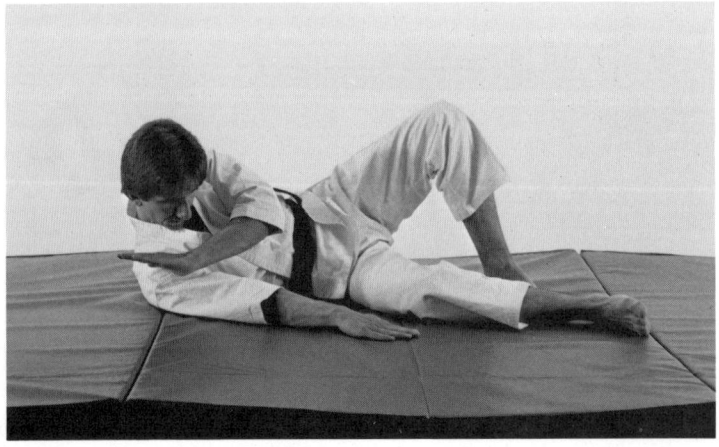

Roll Fall

This technique allows you to fall forward without harming vital areas of the body. Begin in a kneeling position on the mat. Tuck your chin in toward your chest. Slide one arm down to the side as you turn over in a somersault. Beat the palm of your hand against the mat to break your fall just before you land. After some practice, you can try continuing the roll forward and up into a standing position.

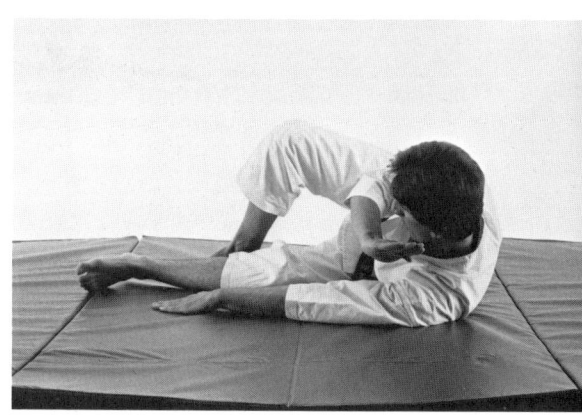

Front Fall

The front fall is useful when someone tackles, sweeps, or throws you forward. You can also use it any time you slip and fall forward. Start in a kneeling position on the mat. Rise up and let your body fall forward. Bring your arms up, the palms facing the mat. Slap the mat with the palms of both hands to break your fall. Your stomach should not touch the mat at any point. It is very important that your hands and arms remain stationary after they slap the mat. They will support your body and will keep it from hitting the mat.

5 MEDITATION

Meditation is an optional exercise that can help cut down on anxiety while clearing the mind and relaxing the body.

The samurai believed that one should prepare for training by first emptying the mind of any tension or unrelated thoughts. This allows the techniques to be more easily learned, with no interference. To accomplish this emptying of mind begin by sitting in the position called *zazen*. In zazen, you sit on the ground with your legs crossed and your hands relaxed and resting upon your bent knees. Relax your shoulders as you stare ahead with your eyes half-closed. Breathe deeply. First, breathe in through the nose and hold for a count of four. Then fully exhale through the mouth. Concentrate on your breathing as you repeat this pattern of deep inhalation and full exhalation. After a while, your mind will clear itself and you will be more relaxed. If your eyelids become heavy, close them. It is very important that while meditating you do not worry about anything. Instead, focus on a spot on the wall with your eyes, concentrate and think about the breathing pattern. If you have trouble doing this, an optional technique used by many is concentration on the number one while breathing. Whenever outside thoughts, worries, or concerns come into your mind, simply focus on the number one and keep thinking about it. Gradually your mind will relax and you will feel clear-headed. After a time, you will come out of this relaxed state by gradually opening your eyes completely and slowly adjusting to an ordinary waking state.

6
FOUNDATION FOR DEFENSE: STANCES

A strong stance is the foundation for self-defense, from which the various blocks, punches, and kicks are performed. If your fighting stances are strong and stable, you will not be easily thrown off balance by an attacker. Your counterattacks will be strong as well. In order to develop a strong stance, you must practice two important principles of jujitsu.

The first principle is that of inner strength. Inner strength is both an awareness of your own inner ability to generate physical power and an ability to control that power. To achieve inner strength, you must focus your thoughts on your lower abdomen (approximately two to two-and-a-half inches below your navel), where your power is centered. This will result in a stance that is very difficult for the aggressor to break. Proper breathing will help you to use your inner strength to its fullest. When you make a defensive move, such as a block or punch, exhale sharply from your lower abdomen.

The other important jujitsu principle involves the power in your hips. When you counterattack, twist your hips in the direction of the attack. This will throw your body weight into the attack and will make your movement very powerful.

Keep these two principles—inner strength and hip power—in mind when you practice the fighting stances. Practice your fighting stances in front of a mirror so you can compare your body positions with those shown in the photographs. Practice each stance until you can assume it almost automatically. When you have learned the individual stances, practice moving quickly and smoothly from one stance to another. By shifting positions, you can take advantage of the special strengths of each particular stance and use the power of each part of your body.

Natural Stance

Face your opponent and stand erect with your feet six to ten inches (about 15 to 25 centimeters) apart. Keep your shoulders relaxed, and let your arms hang comfortably at your sides. Your back should be straight, and your eyes should be focused directly on your opponent.

To assume a right natural stance, begin in the basic natural stance and simply place your right foot forward. For a left natural stance, move your left foot forward from the basic stance. In any natural stance, keep your upper body face forward and your weight evenly distributed over your feet.

NOTE: The natural stance is usually used as the starting position for performing throws. It is very comfortable and you can maintain it for a long time without tiring. You can also shift easily from it to other stances.

Front Stance

This stance is best suited for attack, though it can be used for defense. Stand with the left foot two shoulder-widths forward and to the side of the right foot. Bend the forward leg and let it carry sixty percent of your body weight. Keep your rear leg nearly straight and your heels flat against the ground. Turn your torso toward the opponent. The hands can be held in either low guard or mid-guard position.

NOTE: To assume the low guard, hold your hands in fists at approximately hip level. If you expect to be grappling, hold your front hand open, palm down. Your elbow should be against your ribs to protect them. Tilt both hands slightly up. This guard lets you protect the groin and lower abdomen while keeping your hands in a position from which you can throw very quick reverse and lunge punches.

To assume the mid-guard position, hold both hands open, palm out, at approximately chest level. The elbow should be pointed in toward the ribs. You can make the rear hand into a fist, keeping the front hand open to block or grab. This is for following up blocks with powerful rear punches. The mid-guard position allows you to move quickly to protect either your head or your lower body. It is a compromise position which puts your guard an equal distance from your upper and lower body. A variation that is sometimes used is to keep the forward arm low, at hip level, while the rear arm is in low or mid-guard position. The advantage is that the forward arm can easily block low attacks, while the rear arm blocks blows to the chest and higher.

Back Stance

This stance is used primarily for defense. In this stance, you can easily throw front kicks with the forward leg as the opponent moves in to attack. It is also a very stable stance from which to block.

Stand with one leg in front of the other so that the feet are approximately two shoulder-widths apart. Keep your rear leg deeply bent and let it carry about seventy percent of your weight. Keep your forward leg slightly bent. The hands can be held in either low or mid-guard position.

Horse Stance

This stance allows a person to easily change to any of the other fighting stances. This flexible stance can be used for both defense and attack. It is an especially good stance from which to throw powerful hand attacks.

Stand with your feet apart as if you were riding a horse, with your toes turned slightly inward. Keep your torso erect and your weight evenly distributed over the legs. Variations of this stance are the diagonal and side-facing horse stance. The hands should be made into fists with palms up. The fists are commonly held slightly above the hips in practice, but usually either a low guard or mid-guard hand position is used in combat. Practice this stance with various hand positions so that you can use its full potential.

7
MOVEMENT AND DODGING

Movement and dodging are sometimes very much interconnected. Just shifting from one stance to another is a subtle movement that can be effective in evading attack or mounting an offense. It is best to practice dodging techniques together with body movements so you can learn to move and avoid an attack almost simultaneously. If you practice proper movement and evasion you may not need to try to block certain techniques. As a result, you will not have to absorb the force of the attacker's blow, which can injure you and drain your energy.

DODGES
Stepping-to-the-Rear Dodge

If you are in a natural stance when your opponent attacks, take a step backward so you end in a back stance. To further evade the blow, bend the upper torso slightly to the rear as you move. This dodge can also be used from any of the other fighting stances. For example, if you began in a back stance, step backward with your front foot so it ends behind the other foot. This would put you in a back stance with the opposite foot forward from your original stance.

Leaping Dodge

To perform the technique from a fighting stance, bend your knees and push off to leap away from the attack. Make sure to keep your body loose throughout the movement. Land on the balls of your feet and immediately assume a fighting stance. This dodge can be used to move backwards, off to one side, or even forward and to the side of an attack.

Side Dodge

Begin in a natural stance. Step to the side and bend the upper part of your body away from the attack. If you begin in a fighting stance (such as the back stance), step to the side with your rear foot as you bend your body in that direction. With practice, you will be able to perform side evasions from any stance. It is most important that you end up with your feet to one side of the attacker and your body bent slightly away from the attack.

MOVEMENT
Slide Step

This technique allows you to keep the same foot in front of you as you move forward. It can be done from any of the fighting stances. If you wish to do this technique from a front-facing horse stance, however, you must first take a single step in order to get one foot out in front of the other.

Start in a front stance and slide your front foot forward. Next, slide your back foot forward, until you have regained your original stance. Be sure to maintain proper balance as you move. To move backward, slide your back foot to the rear, then follow with your front foot.

Single Step

This is used to cover a moderate distance quickly. You can use a single step to move forward or backward from any fighting stance. To move forward from a natural stance, simply step forward and to the side with your front foot into a diagonal horse stance. Make sure to maintain proper balance as you step and to keep your upper body erect.

Circle Step

This allows you to move around to an opponent's side or back. It is most often done from a diagonal horse stance or front stance. From one of these stances, move the forward foot eight inches (20 centimeters) to the right or the left, depending on which direction you want to go. Once the forward foot has moved, use it as a pivot to swing the rest of the body in the desired direction. After pivoting, make sure the rear foot is planted firmly on the ground again. At the end of this two-step movement, you should again be in a strong fighting stance. Note the picture illustrates the model moving to his right. He took his first step to the right and then used his stepping foot to swing the rest of his body to the right. To move to the left, he would have stepped to the left with his forward foot and used that foot to pivot the rest of his body.

Cross Step

The cross step is used for very quickly moving the body over a large distance. This technique is also helpful because it tends to confuse the opponent. A cross step is most successful when done from the horse stance. To cross-step to the left, lift your right foot off the ground only slightly, move it quickly in front of the left foot and set it down. At this point your knees should be bent and your feet crossed. In a continuing motion, uncross your feet by moving your left foot farther to the left. This should put you back into a fighting stance. Reverse these movements to step to the right.

THE ART OF ATEMI

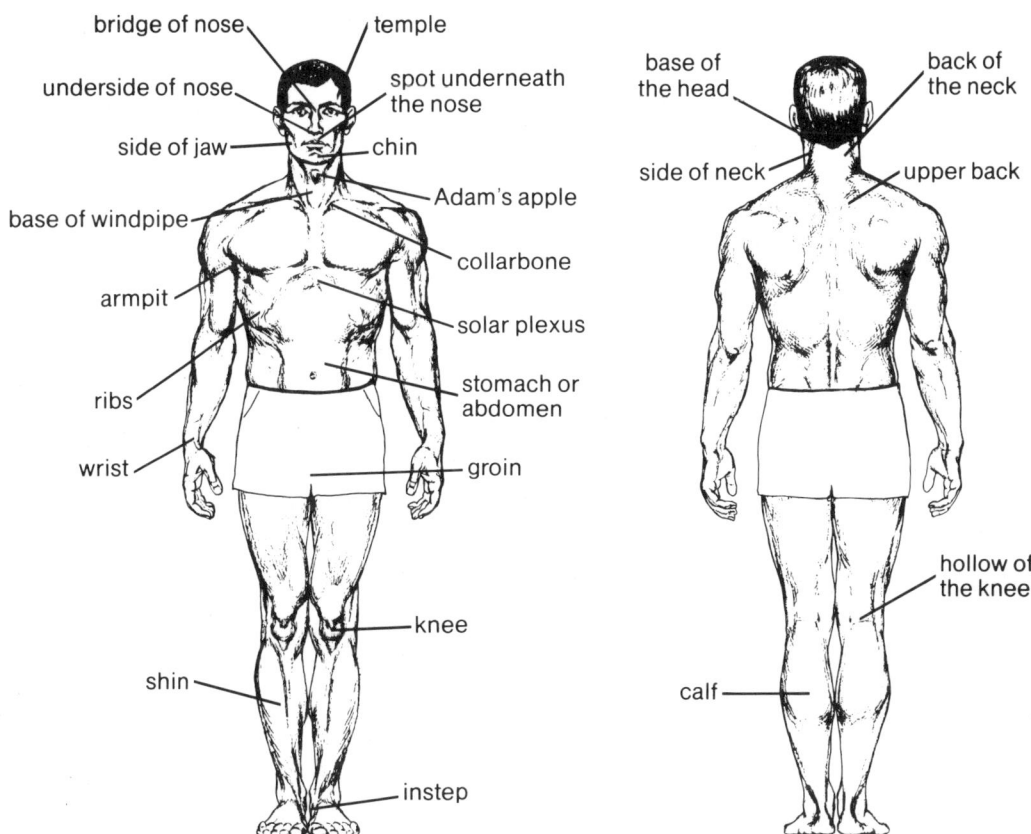

Samurai had various methods of attacking sensitive spots of the body. The art of hitting these weak areas is called *atemi*. Each school of samurai fighting learned the basic spots that would immobilize the attacker when hit. One blow to a sensitive spot may end a fight. It is important, therefore, that you learn these spots and can direct attacks at them. When in close combat, be very aware of these sensitive areas and try to press, hit, or even pinch them. Sometimes it may be necessary to hit two sensitive areas in quick succession. In practice DO NOT use force on a partner. Instead, simply learn where the spots are. Practice contact techniques only against a punching bag or other device.

9

PUNCHES AND STRIKES

The samurai were particularly adept at punching and striking. Each of these techniques gets its power from a particular kind of movement. A punch is a blow that gets its primary power from a thrusting motion. When a punch is thrown, the power moves from the shoulder down into the hand. A strike is a hand technique that gets its power from a snapping motion.

This chapter describes the basic techniques for punching and striking. You must use the proper form for each technique in order to put power into your blow. Before you punch or strike, focus your eyes on the spot you are aiming at. When you concentrate on the target, your blow will be more effective. Remember to exhale for extra power as you deliver the technique, and to twist your hips in the direction of the blow.

It is suggested that you slowly and carefully learn each step in the techniques that follow. Try to compare your form with the illustrations in the book. The better your form, the more likely you will be able to properly deliver the blow in a real fight.

BASIC HAND POSITIONS FOR HITTING

In order to avoid injury and hit most effectively, you should learn to hold your hand correctly when hitting.

Open Hand

Tighten the fingers of your open hand and bend the tips down slightly. Fold the end of the thumb down so that it rests against the palm. Use the outer edge of the hand to make contact with the target.

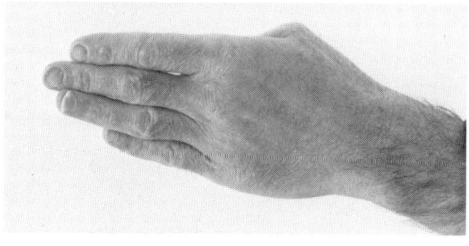

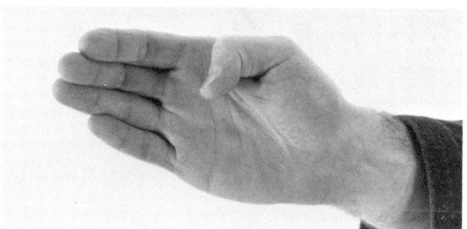

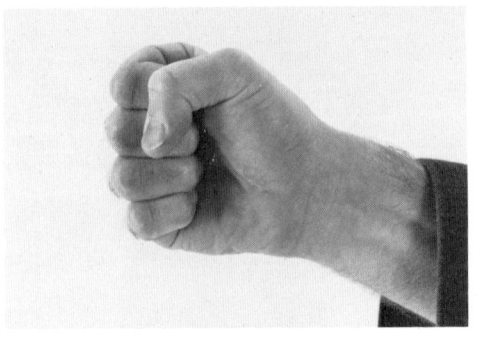

Closed Fist

A proper closed fist is made by tightly folding the fingers into the palm and placing the thumb across the forefinger. The first and second knuckles of the fist should make contact with the target.

An optional method is to tightly fold the fingers into the palm and press the tip of the thumb down tightly on the fingers.

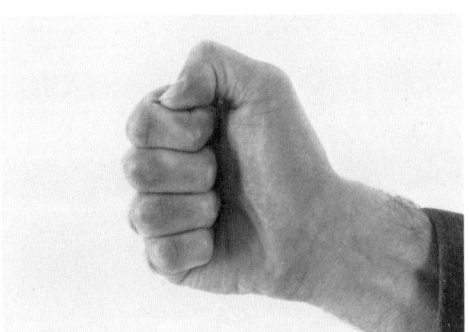

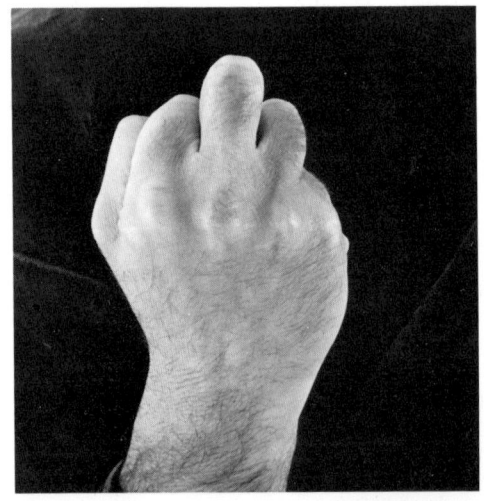

One-Knuckle-Extended Fist

The one-knuckle-extended fist is formed in the same way as the closed fist, except that the middle finger is pushed forward slightly. This knuckle makes contact with the target.

PUNCHES AND STRIKES

Basic Forefist Punch

This is a very powerful technique that can be performed from any of the fighting stances. It can be used to hit an attacker's stomach, chest or head. As this punch is thrown, the fist is twisted to give more power to the attack. To execute the technique, begin in the basic horse stance. Hold your punching hand in a loose fist, palm up, just above your hip. Your other hand should be held out in front of you with the fingers open as if you are grabbing something. Thrust your punching hand forward, twisting your fist quickly. As you hit the target, your palm should face the ground and your knuckles should point forward. Tighten your punching fist just before it hits to add snap and to prevent injury to your hand. For maximum power, pull your other fist back to hip level, palm facing up, as you punch. However, for added protection against a counter-attack, bring this non-punching arm back to a mid-guard position, palm open and facing outward. When maximum flexibility of response is needed for a fast combination of blows, bring the arm back to a vertical position.

Reverse Punch

This very powerful technique can be executed from any stance in which one leg is in front of the other. It is called a reverse punch because the blow comes from the rear side. To execute the technique, reach out with your forward hand as if you were grabbing something. Then twist your rear hip forward and punch quickly with your rear fist. Twist your fist so the palm faces the ground and the knuckles face forward at point of contact. At the same time, bring your other arm back to waist level, palm up. If a counterattack is anticipated, bring the other arm back across the body, palm facing outward, ready to block quickly.

Palm-Up Thrust

This is one of the most effective techniques for penetrating sensitive areas. It is a short thrust that is launched from very close range. It can be thrown from any stance. Simply drive either the open hand like a spear or the closed fist up into the target, palm facing up.

Lunge Punch

This technique has a great deal of power because all of the body weight goes into the punch. It is used to hit the upper part of an opponent's body. The lunge punch is best launched from the diagonal horse stance or front stance. To execute the punch, step forward with your back foot. As it passes your front foot, bring your rear (punching) hand forward in a fist. Your leg and fist should move forward at the same time from the same side of your body. Turn your rear hip toward your opponent as you deliver your punch.

Vertical Punch

This is a very quick technique which can be launched from any stance. Throw your rear fist in a punch, twisting it a quarter-turn. On impact, the thumb side of your fist should be facing up. The other fist is normally pulled back to hip level, palm facing up, as you punch.

Backfist Strike

This powerful strike is used to attack the opponent's head or chest. It is usually executed from the front stance or a form of horse stance. Bring your attacking arm back across your body so the palm of your closed fist is facing your chest. With a quick snap of the elbow, bring your forearm up so the back of your fist strikes the target. At the same time, turn your body toward the target by twisting your hips. For maximum stability, keep both heels flat on the ground while throwing the strike. If an opponent seems to be slightly out of range, you may lift the heel of your rear foot to allow your arm to extend farther into the strike.

Open-Hand Strike

This strike is used to hit an aggressor in a sensitive spot. It can be delivered very quickly because in this position your hand moves easily and quickly through the air. It can be launched from a variety of positions. The key to this strike is a snapping motion from the elbow. To perform one basic open-hand strike, bring your rear hand up by your ear, palm facing outward. Your other hand should be in front of you, palm out, ready to block if necessary. Twist your rear hip forward as your open-palmed hand snaps downward. Twist your wrist so that upon impact the palm is facing up and the side of the hand hits the target. As you strike, the forward arm should be brought back to the hip, palm up.

Elbow Strikes

The elbow strike is very powerful and is a practical strike to use when an attacker is close to you. It can be executed from various angles against an aggressor's body. Make sure you are within striking distance before attempting this technique. It is essential to hit quickly from close to the opponent. The force behind the elbow strike comes from twisting the hip into the strike as well as snapping of the knees. While executing an elbow strike, keep the other arm across the center of your body to protect against a counterattack. The following four variations of the elbow strike can be used for practical self-defense.

Forward Strike

Upward Strike

Sideward Strike

Backward Strike

10
FOOT TECHNIQUES

The samurai used both hand and foot attacks in combat. Hand techniques were fast and powerful and were used at close range. Kicks were coordinated with blows from the hands to catch the opponent off guard or to hit from a distance. To use the kicks taught in this chapter in the most effective way, keep the following principles in mind:
1. Focus your eyes on a target before beginning to kick.
2. Keep the supporting leg slightly bent and planted on the ground.
3. Maintain proper balance and stability throughout the kick.
4. Twist the hip into the kick for greater impact.

Front Kick

This is a very powerful technique used to strike the aggressor's shin, knees, groin, or stomach. Most jujitsu kicking techniques are not thrown higher than the stomach because high kicks leave you more vulnerable to an attacker. Only advanced students should use high kicks.

To perform the basic front kick, begin in any stance. Bend the knee of your kicking leg and lift it toward your chest. Curl your toes upward so they will not be injured when your foot hits the target. Snap your kicking leg forward from the knee and hit the target with the ball of your foot.

Side Kick

This very effective counterattack can be used mostly to hit an aggressor's knees, groin, stomach, or chest. Because of the length of the leg when extended in the side kick, this is ideal for hitting an attacker while staying outside his or her reach. It is most often launched from a side-facing horse stance, but can be used from other stances as well.

Bend the knee of your kicking leg and lift it toward your chest. Be sure your toes are turned upward. Thrust your kicking leg out to the side of your body and hit the target with the heel of your foot. After the kick is completed, pull your leg back to a coiled position. If no further kicks are needed then lay your foot down. After you become skilled in this kick, you may launch the side kick in one smooth action and then lay your foot down immediately. By eliminating the deliberate coil before kicking and recoil afterward, you will be able to kick faster and your foot will be harder to grab.

Back Kick

The back kick is used to defend against attacks from the rear. It is very important to maintain stability and balance throughout this kick so you will have enough power to stop an aggressor. This kick can be used from nearly any stance. To perform the technique, turn your head so you can see behind you. At the same time, bend the knee of your kicking leg and lift it toward your chest. Thrust the kicking leg directly behind you with a snapping motion. The heel of your foot should hit the target. Return to a bent-knee position and, if no further kicks are needed, return to your stance.

Side Ground Kick

This kick is useful if you are thrown to the ground but your aggressor is still standing. Position yourself on your side. Bend the knee of your top leg and draw it tightly to your body. Shoot your leg out as you draw your other leg back to a coiled position to protect your groin. The heel of your foot should contact the aggressor's knee, groin, or lower stomach.

11
BLOCKS

The samurai warriors used a variety of blocks to defend against different attacks. These blocks are more combat-oriented than sport-oriented; each block is generally followed by a grab to immobilize the attacker's limb. Generally, an attack is blocked with the arm closest to the aggressor's attacking limb. The goal is not to just block an attack, but to end the fight as quickly as possible. A block should be the start of a series of counterattacks, never just an isolated movement. The illustrations that follow show only the block, which is the key movement. The grab which follows is a spontaneous action that can be learned later in practice with a partner.

Upward Block

Begin in a fighting stance. As the attacker throws a punch to your head, push the arm closest to the attacking limb upward and away from your body so the outward edge of your forearm contacts the attacker's arm. As soon as the attacker's arm is stopped, the fingers of your blocking arm should grab the aggressor's arm.

Upper-Level Block

This block is used to protect the head. It can be performed from any stance. When an attack is thrown to the head, lift the blocking arm over the head, elbow bent, so it intersects and deflects the attack.

Basic Inward Vertical Block

This is very useful in protecting the upper-middle part of your body. It can be performed in any fighting stance. As an attacker's blow is thrown, bring your arm up with the elbow pointed away from your body. Quickly snap the blocking arm inward so the outside edge of your forearm comes into contact with the opponent's blow.

Outward Vertical Block

This block is used to protect against attacks to the upper and middle levels of the body. Begin in a fighting stance. As the attacker throws a blow, clench the hand of your blocking arm into a fist and bring that arm toward the center of your body. Sweep your arm outward to meet the attacker's limb. Keep the elbow of the blocking arm close enough to your body to protect against further attack.

Double Arm Turn Block

This block protects against either powerful attacks or attacks directed at your side. It can be performed in any stance. As the attack is launched, turn at the waist and swing your upraised arms, underside outward, to meet and deflect the attack.

Downward Block

This block is used to protect the chest, stomach, and groin from attack. It can be used from any fighting stance. Make your forward hand into a fist and position it near the ear on the rear side of your head. Bring the forward arm down to a little below your chest. The outer edge of your forearm should come in contact with the opponent's limb and sweep it away from the body.

Cross Block

The cross block is effective for stopping attacks directed to any part of the body. It can be executed from any fighting stance. To execute the technique, make your hands into fists. Cross your arms and push them to meet the attack. The attacker's hand or leg should be caught between your fists. Try to keep the top half of your body as straight as possible to maintain balance.

12 COMBINATIONS

The samurai believed in smooth, free-flowing action, moving from one technique to another. At times, one blow will not penetrate the defenses of an attacker, and you will need to follow up with another technique. To prepare for this, you should develop strong sets of blows that flow from one to the next, called combinations.

Combinations will give you confidence and the ability to deal with even a skilled attacker. The combinations below are those most commonly used. Practice them until you can do them with grace, power, and speed. In a real fight, do not perform them mechanically, but adapt the movements to fit your needs.

Front kick, right reverse punch

Lift your left leg and kick out to the opponent's stomach. If your opponent moves to block it, drop your foot to the ground and launch a punch to the opponent's head with your right hand. If the front kick lands, it may be unnecessary to follow through with the punch. In circumstances where the opponent steps back to avoid the front kick, you may lift your rear heel to get added reach while performing the reverse punch.

Front kick, reverse punch, forefist punch

Shift your weight to your back leg and lift your front leg, knee bent, toward your chest. Shoot out a left front kick toward the opponent's body. Drop your foot back to the ground and throw a right reverse punch, followed quickly by a left forefist punch.

Side kick, right front kick, reverse punch

Begin in a front stance. Turn to the side and lift your left leg upward, knee bent. Launch your side kick to the aggressor's stomach. After kicking, drop your foot back to the ground. Lift your right (rear) leg toward your chest, knee bent, and kick toward the opponent's body. Then return your leg to its original position. Immediately launch a right reverse punch from the same side of the body.

Fake front kick, lunge punch, sweep

Lift your forward leg as though to throw a kick. When the attacker's guard drops to protect against the kick, lunge forward with a high punch to the head. Your front foot should land behind the opponent's as you lunge. Now push your arm against the opponent's upper body to sweep the person over your leg and off his or her feet.

13
THE ART OF THROWING

The samurai were experts in the art of grappling. Some of their throws were very dynamic, while others were so subtle that you could not see what had happened, except that the attacker landed on the ground. There is no secret to these techniques. They require a lot of skill, gained through hard work and practice.

Throws can be executed from any stance, but are most often initiated from the natural stance. Observe the aggressor's stance carefully and attempt your throw at the exact moment the aggressor is off balance. Keep your body loose and respond quickly to the attacker's movements. The aggressor is always easiest to throw in the direction in which he or she is moving. If an aggressor is not off-balanced by his or her movement, you can break the person's balance by directing the movement. If the aggressor pushes, you should pull. If the aggressor pulls, you should push. An opponent's balance can be broken in eight directions: straight forward, forward to the left, straight to the left, backward to the left, straight backward, backward to the right, straight to the right, forward to the right. Throw your opponent in the direction the person's balance is broken.

The key factors in a successful throw are distance, timing, speed, breathing and balance. You must be able to attack from close range, grasping and sweeping simultaneously. You must be alert and ready to attack the instant the opponent is off balance.

In order to be efficient at jujitsu, you must learn a variety of throws to use against particular kinds of attacks. Practice every throw carefully until the movements become a smooth, automatic response to an attack. It is a good idea to practice the movements alone in front of a mirror so you can compare your body positions and movements to those shown in this chapter. Later, you will also need to practice with a partner. When you practice, follow these essential safety rules:

1. Always do the complete sequence of warm-up exercises before each session.
2. Practice on a large, thick mat designed for falling.
3. Do not practice throws until you and your partner have mastered falling techniques.
4. Do not try to catch your practice partner by surprise. Warn him or her before you attempt a throw.
5. Remember to break an opponent's balance before attempting a throw.

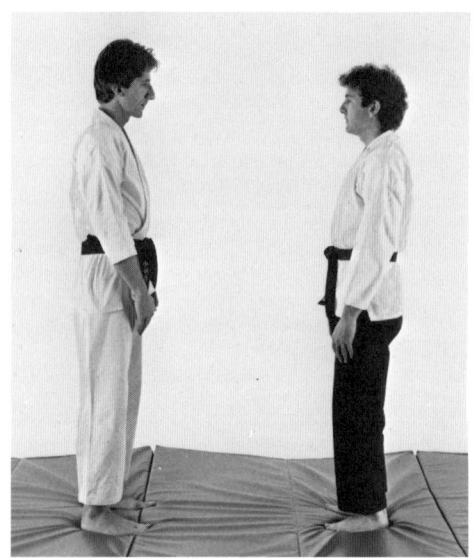

One-Armed Shoulder Throw

This is a powerful defense against an opponent who moves forward to attack or throw you. It is especially useful for a short person against a taller opponent. Begin in a natural stance, facing your opponent. As he or she moves forward, place your right foot in front of the opponent's right foot. At the same time, grasp his or her right arm with your left hand. Pivot on your right foot and step with your left foot so your back is turned toward the opponent. Both knees should be deeply bent when you reach this position. As you pivot, pull the opponent's right arm forward and fit your right arm under the person's armpit. Grab the opponent's shoulder with your right hand. Once the opponent is on your back and ready to throw, finish by springing up, forcing your hips back into the opponent's body, as you pull the person forward over your shoulder.

Scooping Throw

This versatile throw can be used in many situations. It is especially useful when an opponent has a strong hold on you. Begin in a natural stance facing your opponent. Pivot and bring your body around so you are standing to the side of the person. Place your right foot behind the opponent's right foot, and your left foot to the outside of his or her left foot. Bring your right arm across the front of the opponent's body and get a firm grip on the person's leg. At the same time, grab his or her left leg with your left arm. Finally, push your hips forward to off-balance the opponent and lift his or her legs off the mat with your hands.

Big Hip Throw

The big hip throw is one of the basic throws of jujitsu. It is most useful when an opponent is close to you and has a tight grip on your clothing. It may also be used when an opponent is trying to push you backward. Begin in a natural stance and grasp your opponent's right arm with your left hand. Place your right foot next to the inside of the opponent's right foot. At the same time put your right arm around the opponent's waist. Pivot on your right foot and step back with your left foot. The front of the opponent's body will be resting against the back of your hip. At this point your knees should be deeply bent and your toes pointed outward. To finish, spring up and pull the opponent over your hip.

Inside Sweep

This is a very powerful technique to use when an opponent is standing close to you with his or her feet wide apart. Begin by facing the opponent. Grasp both of the person's arms and push backward in order to break his or her balance to the rear. Twist your right hip forward and place your right leg between the opponent's legs so your foot rests behind the person's left foot. Continue pushing the opponent backward and sweep the person's left leg out from under him or her with the back of your right leg.

Springing Hip Throw

This is a most versatile throw because it can be used in a variety of situations in which the opponent would not expect a throw. For example, if the attacker throws a left jab, step forward with your rear foot and block the opponent's punch with an upper-level block. Immediately thereafter, grab the opponent's shoulder as you pivot on your forward foot, bringing your rear foot back a step so the heels of your feet are very close together. Then extend your right foot straight across the opponent's legs. Your left leg should be deeply bent. Your left arm should grab the opponent's right arm and pull it tightly across the body. To throw the opponent, twist the upper part of your body to the left and sweep your right leg back forcefully. At the same time, pull the opponent's right arm to the left and downward across your body.

Basic Foot Sweep (Against a Forward Attack)

This is an excellent technique for catching an opponent off guard. It is often used as a counterattack against an attempted throw. When the opponent steps forward, grab both of his or her arms and place the sole of your rear foot against the outside of the person's heel. To execute the throw, pull down hard on the opponent's arms and sweep the person's foot so he or she falls to the mat. To execute the technique correctly, you MUST act at the exact moment your opponent steps forward, as the weight shifts from one foot to the other but before the person's foot solidly touches ground again.

Cross-Step, Backfist, Sweep

Move in toward your opponent by crossing your left foot behind your right as you begin a backfist at your opponent. If the opponent bends away from the blow, bring your right foot forward behind the opponent's legs so that you are in a horse stance. Place your right arm across the opponent's chest and your left hand near his or her stomach. Push your opponent down and back over your leg. If necessary you may sweep your leg upward to give added motion to your throw. You must begin this technique from a stance which is the opposite of your opponent's. That is, if your opponent has the left foot forward, you would begin with your right foot forward, as shown.

Inner-Thigh Leg Sweep

When an opponent has a very strong forward position, this sweep can very effectively break his or her balance. As your opponent moves forward to attack, cross your right (rear) foot before your forward leg. Reach up and grab the person's arms as you place all your weight on your left foot. Shift all your weight to your left leg and lift your right foot in a circular motion. Strike the opponent's forward leg in the inner thigh area as you grab the person's shoulder in your right hand. The back of your leg should throw the opponent off balance to the front. If you also grab the opponent's arm with your left hand and twist the upper half of your body as you sweep your leg back, you will throw the person to the ground.

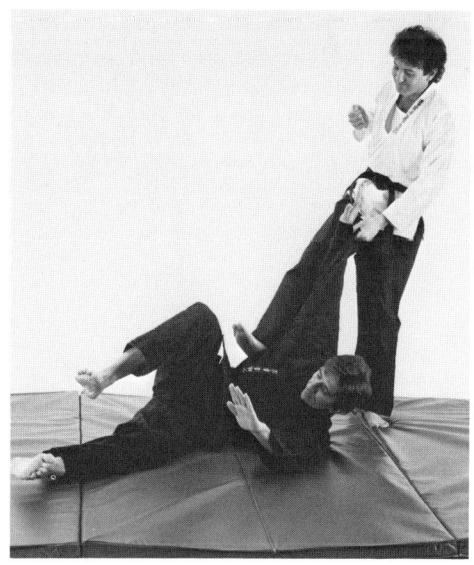

Outside Major Sweep (Against a Front Kick)

If your opponent approaches and attempts to kick you, step to the inside with your forward leg and bend away from the kick. When your opponent's leg is fully extended, reach your left (forward) arm underneath the kicking leg and bring it up. Step forward with your right leg, locking it behind the person's supporting leg. Pull up on your opponent's kicking leg as you sweep back against his or her stationary leg, throwing the attacker to the ground.

Reverse Spin Sweep

As the opponent throws a kick, bring your left arm up underneath the kicking leg and grab it. Your body should be on the outside of the person's kicking leg. Swing your body around by pivoting on your left foot as your right leg swings behind the attacker. Grab the opponent's body with your right hand and sweep back with your right foot against the person's left (stationary) leg, throwing your opponent to the ground.

Rear Leg Sweep

If an opponent is close to you, grab the person's arm and step forward. Pull down on the arm while pushing the person's body backward. This should break your opponent's balance toward the rear. At the same time, slip your rear leg behind the opponent's rear leg so your leg is pressed tightly against the back of his or her leg. Sweep your leg behind you so it takes the opponent's leg out from under him or her.

Side Kick Throw from the Ground

When you are forced onto the ground and your opponent is standing above you, this technique can be used to throw an attacker. Hook one foot behind the opponent's forward leg while driving your other foot against the same leg just below the knee. Pull with your hooking foot while your kicking leg is thrusting. This will force your opponent to the ground.

14
ESCAPES AND COUNTERS

Certain approaches that are common to all simple escapes can be learned by working through some very simple situations. After you have practiced these escapes try to use similar methods in more difficult situations that you may dream up. For example, you will learn to escape from a handshake simply by pushing in the opponent's thumb and sliding your hand outward. Any time your opponent has a grip on you, you may apply a similar escape by depressing the thumb and pulling away. Try to be as innovative as possible in using your self-defense skills in new situations.

Escape from a crushing handshake

If an attacker has you in a crushing handshake, simply push the attacker's thumb inward with your other hand as you pull the locked hand free. This movement can be used in a variety of situations. To help break the grip, you can pull back on the little finger of the opponent's hand.

Escape from a grip

If the opponent grabs your wrist with one hand, bend your arm at the elbow and bring it quickly toward your chest. Slide your wrist through the gap between the attacker's thumb and fingers. The key is to build momentum and to use the lever action of bending your arm to pull through the attacker's fingers. If necessary, or if your opponent has seized your wrist with both hands, grab your gripped hand with your free hand. Pull upward with your arms and shoulders so your hand breaks through where the opponent's thumbs meet the fingers.

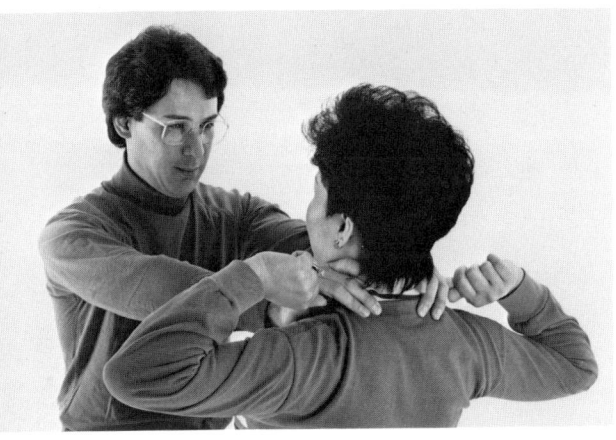

Escape from a two-handed choke

Grab the attacker's little fingers and spread them outward to break the hold.

Escape from a shover

When an opponent shoves you with his or her hands, bring your arms up underneath the person's elbows as you evade to the side with your head. Once your opponent's arms are raised, follow through with a punch to the body.

Escape from a bear hug

There are many variations to the hold commonly known as the bear hug. To escape from a front bear hug with your arms pinned, bring your knee up into the attacker's groin, bring one of your knees up against your opponent's knee and press forward with all your weight, or pinch your opponent's inner thigh area. You may use the space between you to throw a hand attack.

When grabbed around the waist from behind, beat on the back of the attacker's hand with an extended knuckle. Next, step to the right and bend down. Push your hips back and grab the opponent's right leg with both hands. Lift the attacker's leg upward while pressing against it with the back of your thigh.

When you are grabbed from behind and your arms are pinned, inhale to expand your body. Pinch hard against the person's thigh as you exhale and step off to the side. Another alternative is to exhale and kick back at the opponent's knee. You can apply a lock to end the confrontation. Remember, never use full force or complete a kick against a practice partner.

Escape and wristlock counter from a front grip

Grab the person's wrist and turn his or her arm over with a quick action. This will force the opponent's arm into a barred position, causing pain in the person's elbow and wrist.

Escape from a full nelson

If an opponent has you in a full nelson, lift both arms high and place one hand on your forehead with the palm facing outward and the other, palm outward, on top of it. Press back to relieve the pressure on your neck. Suddenly shoot your arms straight up, then bring your elbows down hard as you bend your knees deeply. This should be one quick, continuous motion. If the opponent has loosened the hold, straighten slightly and bring one of your knees up, then kick back at your opponent's shins.

Escape when pinned on the ground

If you are prone with the attacker pinning you, push the person up and forward by arching your hips off the ground. At the same time, raise your arms straight over your head. The attacker should move his or her hands to block the fall. When the opponent does so, throw the person off by twisting up and to the side. To contain the attacker, swing on top of the attacker as you pin the person's arm behind him or her.

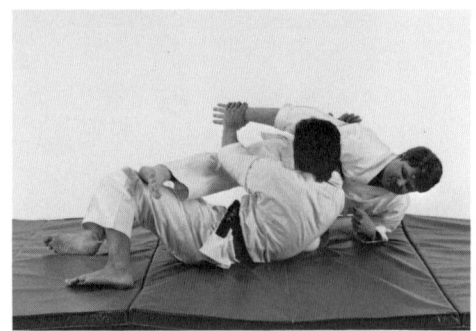

Block and armbar combination against a punch

When an opponent throws a punch at you, block, grab, and follow up by slipping your other arm around the opponent's punching arm. Press back against the opponent's arm at the wrist and elbow.

Escape from front headlock

If you are in the front headlock or what is often known as the "sweatbox," first bend your knees quickly. At the same time, thrust your right arm around the opponent's arms to grab the hair at the back of the person's head. Pull hard as you twist to break free. Once you are free, apply a simple locking technique by pulling the opponent's choking arm straight across your body, pressing back hard against the elbow.

Escape from side headlock

Bend your knees deeply as you bring the arm closest to the opponent around the person's shoulder and underneath his or her nose. Even a light blow to this sensitive area of the nose should force the attacker to loosen the hold so you can escape. Once free, step forward and bring the arm that delivered the blow down to where the opponent's upper arm meets his shoulder. Meanwhile pull upward on the person's wrist with your other hand. Finish with a straight armlock, putting pressure on the wrist and elbow of the opponent.

Wristlocks

Wristlocks are very powerful tools in self-defense. They allow a small person to overcome a powerful assailant. They put pressure on the wrist, which is extremely sensitive.

You must keep this sensitivity in mind when either stretching the wrist or applying a wristlock in practice. The moment your partner appears to be uncomfortable, the lock should be released, even if your partner does not say anything. It is very important that you and your partner work out a signal that tells you to release a lock. Beginning students should simply go through the actions with a partner who is standing still and not resisting. Wristlocks should be practiced only under supervision at first.

Wristlocks are most often applied when an opponent is either reaching for you or is in a position where one hand is still and easy to grab. A wristlock must be applied smoothly, quickly, and without hesitation in order to be effective. In practice, however, you must move slowly in order to make sure you have the proper form and are not applying needless pressure to a partner. Do not attempt to throw or to force a partner to the ground with a wristlock. Even advanced students of jujitsu allow a partner to ease down to the floor when practicing throws which use wristlocks. Remember, a practice session is not a fight or an opportunity to show how tough you are. Your sincerity and ability will be gauged by your attention to form and safety and your concern for others.

A. Inward Wristlock

Swing the opponent's hand up and inward in a semicircle toward your shoulder. This forces the opponent's hand to face him or her, palm inward and thumb outward.

B. Outward Wristlock

Grab the opponent's arm and swing it outward so the palm of the hand is facing down and out.

15
CONTAINMENT STRATEGY

STRATEGIC CONCERNS

Certain concepts shared by many of the samurai schools of fighting will be discussed in this chapter. Each jujitsu student must study and practice and then bring together those fighting strategies that best fit his or her needs. This means each person will defend himself or herself differently. There is no one method that can be memorized or one strategy that will always work against every attacker. Presence of mind, ability to adapt, and the proper execution of technique all play a part in ensuring success. Think through the following strategies and incorporate them in your practice. Knowledge is only potential power. Real power comes from the application of knowledge.

Use your number one asset—your mind.

Nothing is more important in self-defense than the power of the mind.

Muscle power cannot substitute for proper thinking. Therefore, it is important that you learn to control your mind and emotions as well as your body. Concentrate on what you are doing. Power is multiplied when all energy is focused on one task.

Use strategy to win.

Plan a strategy when dealing with an attacker. Do not simply charge ahead without thinking. Consider the attacker's sensitive spots, weaknesses, strengths, openings, and balance as you move ahead. Never allow anger to control your actions, but instead rely on strategy.

Break an aggressor's balance.

Every movement an attacker makes will leave the person briefly open or off balance. The samurai were experts in the art of off-balancing an attacker. When a person's balance is uncertain, he or she can easily be thrown or outmaneuvered. Watch an opponent's stance to see how the person is balanced. A throw should be attempted at the exact moment an opponent is off balance.

Take advantage of a gap.

Opponents often have a momentary lapse, sometimes known as *suki*. This happens when they are distracted, or have just finished a technique or are catching their breath. During that lapse of time, even the strongest opponent can be countered. For example, if an opponent throws a punch and misses you, for an instant that person will still be concentrating on movement. If you launch your counterattack at an open spot before the opponent has recovered, there is great likelihood of success.

Create illusion and confusion.

It is important to distract your opponent and keep him or her confused. If your opponent does not know what to expect next, you can easily overcome that person. Distraction will give you time to break a hold or counterattack. Confusing the attacker may make the difference between successfully defending yourself and being seriously injured. You can distract an opponent by yelling, throwing an object, or faking one attack as you launch another. An example of this would be throwing your fist as if to punch while following with a kick to the opponent's shin. Distracting and confusing techniques should be practiced constantly.

Be flexible in your responses to any situation.

No matter how many techniques you learn, they will always have to be adapted to a specific confrontation. You must keep an open mind and be able to put together different combinations of blows, escapes, and throws. In practices, imagine an attacker doing a variety of things, and see how you can adapt what you know to meet the situation. If you develop a flexible mind, you will be able to more adequately defend yourself.

TYPES OF DEFENSES

There are three types of defenses used by the samurai in confrontations. They are the instant attack, the waiting attack, and the body-to-body attack.

Instant Attack

In an instant attack, you move toward an aggressor as soon as a confrontation begins, attacking before your opponent can harm you. This attack is only used when a bully clearly intends to fight and there is no way you can back off. You may then have to seize the initiative by striking any opening that is available. However, use force only when it is clear by the attacker's actions that he or she means to harm you, and use only a reasonable amount of force. An excellent time to launch an instant attack is when your opponent is distracted. Once you decide on this strategy, you must not hesitate.

With the instant attack, you take the initiative. It is a way to physically outmaneuver an opponent and seize a psychological edge. The instant attack is not an excuse to start a fight, but only a defensive response.

Waiting Attack

In the waiting attack, the first move your opponent makes leaves an opening or puts the person off balance. You let your opponent expend his or her energy and then you counterattack. If an opponent moves and you dodge, there will be a gap in the action or in your opponent's attention. If you do not hesitate, if you move forward quickly, your counterattack may be devastating enough to end the fight. The waiting attack takes advantage of opponents' rhythms by allowing them to drain away their energy on failed attacks and then

redirecting their own energy against them.

This is probably the most often used samurai fighting technique. Do not, however, become overly dependent on it. It may not always be clear how to take advantage of your opponent's weakness, so another strategy may be necessary. At other times, the attacker may think you are weak because you hold back, and may press the fight. On a bigger scale, you may want to draw out an opponent to force him or her to make a mistake.

Like many of the other lessons of the samurai, these principles may have broader application than just in self-defense.

Body-To-Body Attack

In the body-to-body attack, the opponent makes the initial move, but before the person can land a blow or grab you, you move in and hit or throw the person. An example is when an opponent starts to grab and the defender moves in close to the aggressor's body with a quick combination of blows. The defender's sudden movement nullifies the aggressor's action.

HANDLING SPECIFIC TYPES OF ATTACKERS

Although you must always be flexible in dealing with attackers, certain general strategies can be useful in handling specific types. This section explains how to deal with each type of attacker. Earlier in the book, defenses and escapes against specific techniques were outlined. If you keep in mind the overall strategy for dealing with each type of attacker, the basic samurai defense principles, and the specific techniques, and adapt tactics to fit the situation, your chance of success is very great. Below are the four basic types of attackers that you may face.

1. The Intimidator

Some individuals enjoy picking on someone they believe is weaker and afraid of them. These bullies most likely are uncertain and afraid, and try to build themselves up by bringing somebody down. Just knowing this should give you confidence. This type of bully dreads an individual who is not afraid of physical contact. If you believe you are up against this type of attacker, look the person in the face and show no fear. Keep a safe distance away and be ready for attack. Never beg or threaten. Your sense of self-confidence will impress your attacker and put fear in the person's heart. The minute the bully begins an attack, move against a sensitive spot on the person's body, try to break the person's balance, or block the attack and follow through with a locking technique. An intimidator often backs down when you resist and show no fear. When you strike, hit hard and do not think of defeat.

2. The Shover

Some people constantly push or pull other people because it gives them a sense of power. If they are just being playful and you sense no combative intent, you can simply

laugh it off and walk away. On the other hand, if you sense the shove may lead to something else, carefully watch for a break in the person's

balance, or any openings for attack in sensitive spots or for a lock that you can apply. For example, as suggested in the balance section, if the person pushes you backward, pull forward so he or she is off balance, and follow with a throw. Sometimes just being smart enough to direct the person's energy and put him or her in an awkward position will discourage the attacker. Look at the process as a challenge, not as something to fear.

3. The Grappler

When an individual grabs at you aggressively, you may have to move immediately to defend yourself. First, decide whether you can simply walk away and avoid further problems or whether you need to take action. If you cannot move away from the attacker, try to dodge and follow through with a blow of your own. Once the fight begins, never move directly forward into an attacker's reach. Although a powerful punch may be enough to drop one opponent, the same blow may have a different effect on another adversary. Some grapplers may be willing to take a blow in order to get the opportunity to grab you and wrestle you to the ground.

When first sizing up such an individual, you must move around and watch for openings. Try to hit the opponent on the side of the body so you are outside the person's easy reach. Don't throw high kicks that will leave you off balance. Any kick should

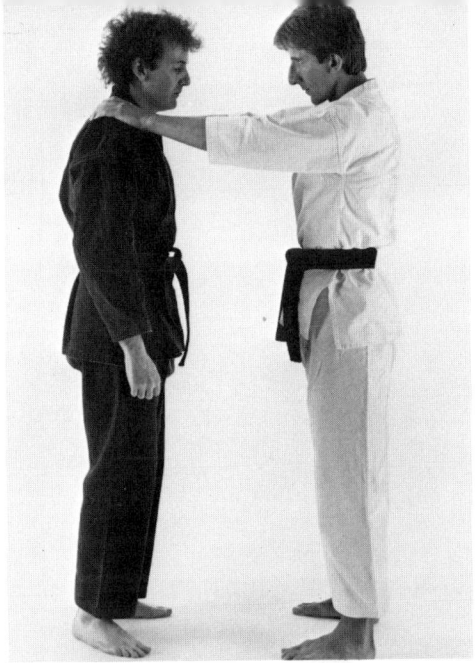

then withdraw. Elbow strikes are very effective for close combat. If the opponent grabs you, the grip can be broken by bending the person's little finger back, striking at a sensitive spot, or pinching. It is amazing how a pinch in a tender area can force the most powerful attacker to let go.

The grappler often stands stationary while trying to force you to the ground. If caught in the grappler's hold, quickly apply a lock that will contain the person. Do not become discouraged when dealing with this type of opponent. Instead, plan a strategy that will keep you out of grappling range but let you hit sensitive spots. If you have confidence in your throwing abilities, do not hesitate to attempt a throw—IF the attacker is off balance.

be quick and no higher than the opponent's knee. If you are forced into very close range, try to hit any sensitive area that is open for attack, and

4. The Aggressive Puncher

Some bullies do intend to harm you and are not afraid to fight it out. Don't fear this type of individual, but instead manipulate the person with strategy. This attacker's skill is most likely low, and the person depends on winning by continued attacks which take a toll on the victim.

When confronted by such a bully, stay away until you can assess the pattern of attack. Develop a plan and then use it. Do not waste energy with attacks that are not part of your plan. If you are stronger than your opponent or confident of your grappling skills, maneuver the opponent to close range and perform a lock or throw. Otherwise, stay mobile and wear down your aggressor with attacks to the front and side.

If the opponent puts his or her head down and starts swinging, then you can drive a hard kick to the person's body or groin. This allows you to stay at a safe range and hit your opponent without him or her hitting you. The best kick for this is the side kick because of its length of reach.

If the opponent uses more sophisticated tactics in his or her hand attacks, simply evade to one side so the attack misses. Then follow through with a quick combination of hand attacks. If you get caught in a grappling hold, use an escape, a hold, or a throw. Often such individuals are easily caught off guard by simple holds. The aggressive fighter who is not used to an intelligent opponent will be discouraged by a persistent defense.

16
SAFETY CONSIDERATIONS

The arts of the samurai can be exciting to practice. They can build confidence and improve your health, provided you practice with proper care. A practice session is not a real fight or an opportunity to take advantage of your partner's weakness. Instead, it is a chance to build your skill and develop cooperation with others. Proper safety precautions should always be followed to avoid injury. The following safety tips should be kept in mind throughout each and every practice session for as long as you study the art.

1. Practice when you are not upset or tired. Your body must be loose and you must have enough energy to perform the techniques properly.
2. Perform warm-up exercises and

stretches before each training session. At the end of your practice of fighting techniques, finish with a set of cool-down exercises.
3. Don't be in a hurry to stretch your muscles. A slow series of stretches will do more for your body than quick calisthenics. Be patient with your body and do not expect it to stretch out in one day. Sometimes it takes months to get the body into condition when you are first beginning to train. It is better to do an exercise slowly than do too much at once and risk an injury.
4. Do not hit a partner in practice. All blows should be stopped at least one inch (2.5 centimeters) from your partner's body. Punches, strikes, or kicks should be practiced on the punching bag. Only very advanced jujitsu practitioners, under the supervision of an instructor, are allowed to make moderate contact on one another.
5. Never surprise your partner with a throw, sweep, block, or hold in practice. Be sure your partner is ready to start before executing these techniques. Become proficient at falling techniques before attempting any throws. It is also important that any throw is done on a safety mat.
6. Make sure you and your partner are warmed up, well stretched, and loose before applying any locking techniques or holds.
7. Work out a warning system with your partner to signal one another if a hold or lock is painful, so you can release immediately.
8. Practice holds, locks, or throws that are new to you only under the supervision of a qualified martial arts instructor.

Index

ankle conditioners, 31
atemi, 51

back kick, 63
back stance, 44
back-stretching exercise, 30
backfist strike, 59
balance, breaking an opponent's, 25, 75, 102
big hip throw, 78
block and armbar combination, 97
body-to-body attack, 104
body-twisting exercise, 29
Buddhism, 12-13, 24
bushi, 11
Bushido, 10, 14, 17-21

circle step, 49
closed fist, 54
conditioning, 23, 27
cross block, 68
cross step, 50
cross step, backfist, sweep, 82

daimyo, 11
double arm turn block, 67
downward block, 68

elbow strikes, 60
escapes: and wristlock counter from a front grip, 94; from a bear hug, 92-93; from a crushing handshake, 89; from a front headlock, 98; from a full nelson, 95; from a grip, 90; from a shover, 91; from a side headlock, 99; from a two-handed choke, 91; when pinned on the ground, 96

falling exercises, 35-38
foot sweep against a forward attack, 81
forefist punch, 55
front fall, 38
front kick, 61
front stance, 42

hip power, 41
horse stance, 44

inner strength, 41
inner-thigh leg sweep, 83
inside sweep, 79
instant attack, 103
inward vertical block, 66
isshin, 20

judo, 9
jujitsu: civilian, 14; combat, 9, 14; defined, 14

karate, 24-25
kempo, 13
ki, 26
kufu, 21

leaping dodge, 46
low guard, 43
lunge punch, 57

makoto, 20
Meiji restoration, 14-15
mid-guard, 43
mushin, 20

natural stance, 42
neck conditioner, 28

one-armed shoulder throw, 76
one-knuckle-extended fist, 54
open hand, 53
outside major sweep against a front kick, 84
outward vertical block, 67
palm-up thrust, 56

rear fall, 35

rear leg sweep, 86
reverse punch, 56
reverse spin sweep, 85
roll fall, 37

samurai: armor, 12-13; skills, 12; weapons, 12
scooping throw, 77
sensitive spots, 51
Shinto religion, 24
shogun, 11
side dodge, 47
side fall, 36
side ground kick, 63
side kick, 62
side kick throw from the ground, 87
side stretch, 28
single step, 48
slide-step, 48
springing hip throw, 80
stepping-to-the-rear dodge, 46
suki, 21, 102
sumai, 11

toe touches, 28
Tokugawa era, 14
two-leg stretch, 29

upper-level block, 66
upward block, 65

vertical punch, 57

waiting attack, 103-104
wall push-up, 30
warrior monks, 12
way of the warrior, 14, 17-21
wrist circle, 32
wrist stretch, 33
wrist, hand, and forearm conditioner, 34
wristlocks, 94, 100

zazen, 39
Zen Buddhism, 12-13, 18, 24

About the Author

Fred Neff started his training in the Asian fighting arts at the age of eight and eventually specialized in karate. In 1974, Mr. Neff received a rank of fifth degree black belt in karate. The same year he was made a master of the art of kempo at a formal ceremony. He is also proficient in judo and jujitsu. Mr. Neff's study of Oriental culture has taken him to such lands as Hong Kong, Japan, the People's Republic of China, and Singapore.

For many years, Mr. Neff has used his knowledge to help and educate others. He has taught karate at the University of Minnesota, the University of Wisconsin, Hamline University and Inver Hills College in St. Paul, Minnesota. He has also organized and supervised self-defense classes for special education programs, public schools, private institutions, and city recreation departments. Included in his teaching program have been classes for law enforcement officers.

He has received many awards for his active community involvement, including the City of St. Paul Citizen of the Month Award in 1975, a Commendation for Distinguished Service from the Sibley County Attorney's Office in 1980, the WCCO Radio Good Neighbor Award in 1985, and the Lamp of Knowledge Award from the Twin Cities Lawyers Guild in 1986.

Fred Neff graduated with high distinction from the University of Minnesota College of Education in 1970. In 1976, he received his J.D. degree from William Mitchell College of Law in St. Paul, Minnesota. Mr. Neff is now a practicing attorney in Minneapolis, Minnesota.

He is the author of fourteen books, including *Everybody's Book of Self-Defense, Karate is for Me, Lessons from the Western Warriors, Lessons from the Art of Kempo, Lessons from the Samurai,* and the eight books which make up Fred Neff's Self-Defense Library.

LIBRARY
Davies Career & Technical H.S.
Lincoln, R.I. 02865